Our World

LIVE. LEARN. DISCOVER.

PaRRagon

Bath · New York · Singapore · Hong Kong · Cologne · Delhi · Melbourne

Our World

Take an amazing journey through human civilization

Author: Steve Parker

First published by Parragon in 2008
Parragon
Queen Street House
4 Queen Street
Bath BA1 1HE, UK

Copyright © Parragon Books Ltd 2008

ISBN 978-1-4075-4459-5
Printed in China

Index

Index

Acknowledgments

Artwork

David Lewis Illustration: 23CL Peter Visscher, 31TR Bruce Hogarth, 33C,TL Bruce Hogarth, 34–35CRCL Bruce Hogarth, 37C Bruce Hogarth, 39TL Bruce Hogarth, 41CL Bruce Hogarth, 43CLCR Bruce Hogarth, 46TR Bruce Hogarth; **Precision Illustration:** 59TL Tim Loughhead, 67T Tim Loughhead, 74BR Tim Loughhead, 77TL Tim Loughhead, 79TL Tim Loughhead, 81BC Tim Loughhead, 89TL Tim Loughhead, 91TL Tim Loughhead

Photography

Photo credits:
B—bottom, T—top, R—right, L—left, C—center

Alvey & Towers: 84BR; **CLAAS:** 80–81CRCL; **Corbis:** cover TR Rob Howard, cover BR Liu Liqun, poster Bryan Allen, 6-7C Press-Telegram/Steven Georges, 9CL epa/Robin Utrecht, 9BR Peter Turnley, 11TR Michael Wray, 12TL David Turnley, 13CL Zefa/G. Baden, 14BR Stock Photos/Zefa/Lance Nelson, 15BR Louie Psihoyos, 17T Robert Harding World Imagery, 17BR Zuma/Art Stein, 18TL James Marshall, 18BR Wolfgang Kaehler, 19BR Liu Liqun, 20TL Zefa/Stefan Schuetz, 20BL Zefa/Herbert Kehrer, 20TR Zefa/Alexander Hubrich, 21B Creasource, 22BR Kazuyoshi Nomachi, 23TR Reuters/Gaby Sommer, 23BR Robert Harding World Imagery/Christian Kober, 24TR Reuters/Reinhard Krause, 24BL Reuters/Brijesh Singh, 25T Sygma/Micheline Pelletier, 27CL Reuters/Seth Wenig, 27TR epa/Royal Household handout, 27BR epa/Narong Sangnak, 29 George Shelley, 30TR Reuters, 30BR Rob Lewine, 31B Zefa/Joson, 32R Zefa/Matthias Kulka, 33BL Jim Craigmyle, 33TR Zefa/Gary Salter, 34BL Steve Prezant, 35R Reuters/Gary Hershorn, 36TR Roy Morsch, 36B Tom & Dee Ann McCarthy, 37TR Stephen Frink, 37BR epa/Marcos Delgado, 38CL dpa/Maurizio Gambarini, 40TL Zefa/Grace, 40BR Patrik Giardino, 41BR Laura Dwight, 42BL Zefa/Mika, 44TR Zefa/René Shenouda, 45CLReuters, 46BL Jim Erickson, 47TR Reuters, 47CL Reuters/Stringer, 48CR Zefa/Grace, 49TR Zefa/Stephen Beaudet, 49BL Zefa/Ole Graf, 49BR Zefa/G. Baden, 54C Larry Williams, 54BL Reuters/Reuters, 54–55BRBL epa/British Petroleum, 55TL Tom & Dee Ann McCarthy, 55R Visuals Unlimited, 56BL James Noble, 59R Zefa/Klaus Hackenberg, 61R Jonathan Blair, 64BL George Hall, 65BR Tom & Dee Ann McCarthy, 66L Paul A. Souders, 67B Natalie Fobes, 70BL Kevin Fleming, 70–71TRCL Paul A. Souders, 71BR Kevin Fleming, 75B Zefa/Ole Graf, 75TL Lester Lefkowitz, 75CR TWPhoto, 78T Royalty-Free, 78BR Reuters, 174TL Zefa/Erika Koch, 174BR Charles O'Rear, 84TL Reuters/Issei Kato, 85B Zefa/Kurt Amthor, 87BR Zefa/Klaus Hackenberg, 88BL epa/Armando Arorizo, 88–89 CCL Handout/Reuters/Airbus Industrie, 91BR Handout/Reuters/Jack Atley, 93C Stuart Westmorland; **Dyson:** 76BL, 76TR; **Getty Images:** coverTL David Rosenberg, cover B Don Smith, coverBC Travel Ink, 1C Bill Reitzel, 2-3 The Image Bank/Robert Holland, 6-7 Robert Glusic 8TL Photonica/Jorg Greuel, 8BR Robert Harding World Imagery/Upperhall, 9TR Stone/Manfred Mehlig, 10L Stone/Nicholas Prior, 11CL Stone/Lawrence Migdale, 11BR ArabianEye, 12BR Getty Image News/Robert Nickelsberg, 13TR Taxi/Gary Buss, 13BR Stone/David Hanson, 14TL Stone/Terry Vine, 15TL Photodisc Green/Ryan McVay, 15TR Photographer's Choice/Ron Levine, 16TL Stone/Gary Yeowell, 16BR Stone/Tony Duffy, 19TL Reportage/Scott Nelson, 19TR Taxi/Rana Faure, 22TL First Light/Huy Lam, 25BR Asia Images/Steve Raymer, 26BL AFP/Lioel Healing, 26TR AFP/Kazuhiro Nogi, 35C Image Bank/Terje Rakke, 38–39BRBL Taxi/Jim Cummins, 39TR Iconica/PM Images, 41TR Photodisc green/PNC, 44B Patrick Bernard, 45TR The Image Bank/Britt Erlanson, 47BR Stone/Don Smetzer, 48L The Image Bank/LWA, 52TL Photodisc Green/Erin Hogan, 52BR Dorling Kindersley, 53TL The Image Bank/Pat LaCroix, 56C Photodisc Green/Robert Glusic, 57B Science Faction/Louie Psihoyos, 58C Aurora/Jim Thornburg, 58–59BRBL Photonica/Henrik Sorensen, 60TR The Image Bank/Joseph Van Os, 60BL Workbook Stock/Bromberger-Hoover, 61BL Stone/Robert Frerck, 62TL Taxi/Photo & Co, 62BL Stone/David Davies, 62-63CRTL Stone/Doug Armand, 63CR Taxi/Tyler Stableford, 64C Photonica/Roberto Mettifogo, 66CR Stone/Michael Rosenfeld, 68TR Photodisc Green/Erin Hogan, 73 The Image Bank/Robert Holland, 74TL Taxi/Dana Neely, 79BR Taxi/Nick Dolding, 80BL Stone/Graeme Norways, 81TR Stone/Bruce Hands, 82BL Photodisc Blue, 83TR The Image Bank/Lester Lefkowitz, 83BL Photodisc Green/Jess Alford, 86C Taxi/Adastra, 86BL Photodisc Blue, 87TL Photonica/Jake Rajs, 89T Stone/Ross Harrison Koty, 89BL Taxi/Jeff Sherman, 90TL Photonica/VEER /Don Johnston, 90–91BRBL Stone/Martin Rogers, 91CR Iconica/Simon Plant; **iStockPhoto:** cover BL Jerry McElroy, 4-5C Jerry McElroy, 7TR GWFlash, 8TL GWFlash, 10TL GWFlash, 12TL GWFlash, 14TL GWFlash, 16TL GWFlash, 18TL GWFlash, 20TL GWFlash, 22TL GWFlash, 24TL GWFlash, 26TL GWFlash, 30TL Macroworld, 32TL Macroworld, 34TL Macroworld, 36TL Macroworld, 38TL Macroworld, 40TL Macroworld, 42TL Macroworld, 44TL Macroworld, 45CL José Luis Gutiérrez, 45C Tyler Olson, 46TL Macroworld, 48TL Macroworld, 51 Jerry McElroy, 53C Trina Denner, 57TR Charles Shapiro, 71TL Bebe Bailey, 74TL Alvaro Heinzen, 76TL Alvaro Heinzen, 77CR Dan Brandenburg, 78TL Alvaro Heinzen, 80TL Alvaro Heinzen, 80TR TexasMary, 82TL Alvaro Heinzen, 82TR BuzBuzzer, 84TL Alvaro Heinzen, 85TL Andrea Leone, 86TL Alvaro Heinzen, 88TL Alvaro Heinzen, 90TL Alvaro Heinzen; **L'Equip:**77BL; **NASA:** 65TR; **Naturepl:** 43TR Hans Christoph Kappel; **Science Photo Library:** 38TR Alfred Pasieka, 42TR Adam Hart-Davis, 42TC Adam Hart-Davis, 53BR Eye of Science, 68C Jeremy Walker; **Scintilla Pictures:** 30BL John Avon, 67C John Avon, 69TR John Avon, 69CR John Avon, 69BR John Avon

96

Skillful flying

Demonstration pilots fly their planes very close together and do tricks, such as spinning and flying upside down. They also fly big circles called "looping the loop."

The demonstration squadron of the U.S. Navy is called the Blue Angels.

A380 AIRBUS

The Airbus 380 is the largest passenger airplane in the world. It can carry up to 840 passengers.

How wings work

Fast moving air lifts wing up.

Wing

To take off, an airplane has to speed along the runway. As it moves, the teardrop shape of its wings forces air to move faster over the top of the wing than under it. This creates suction above the wing that lifts the airplane up into the air.

At the controls

The pilot flies the airplane from the cockpit. In the cockpit of a big passenger airplane, there are hundreds of dials, lights, screens, and controls. A powerful computer called the "automatic pilot" helps the pilot to fly the airplane safely.

Out at sea

Out at sea, ships and boats must find their way carefully. There are no signs to follow and the weather can make the sea rough and dangerous. Ships use radios, or satellites in space, to guide them.

Jet skis

Jet skis are like jet-powered motorcycles you ride on water. They have powerful engines that suck in water and then squirt it out behind in a powerful jet. This pushes the jet ski along at high speed.

Supertankers

The largest boats ever built are called supertankers. They carry oil across the great oceans of the world. They are so big that they take 20 minutes to stop and need over a mile of sea to turn around in.

Hydrofoils

Hydrofoils are boats that can rise up out of the water on special wings called foils. When moving slowly, the hydrofoil looks like an ordinary boat. But as it goes faster, it rises up onto its foils. It can then go even faster.

At high speed the hydrofoil rises out of the water.

Foils

Sailboats

Sailboats are blown along by the wind. If the wind is very strong, the boat sometimes leans right over. As the wind changes direction, the "crew," or people working on the boat, pull ropes to change the direction of the sails to catch the wind.

This large sail is called a spinnaker.

1030

Quick Quiz

Find the correct stickers to answer the questions below!

Which of these household machines works using suction?

washing machine

can opener

vacuum cleaner

Answer

Which of these forms of transportation is wind-powered?

Answer

sailboat

jet ski

supertanker

Which of these simple machines would you not find on a bicycle?

ramp

gears

wheel

Answer

Contents

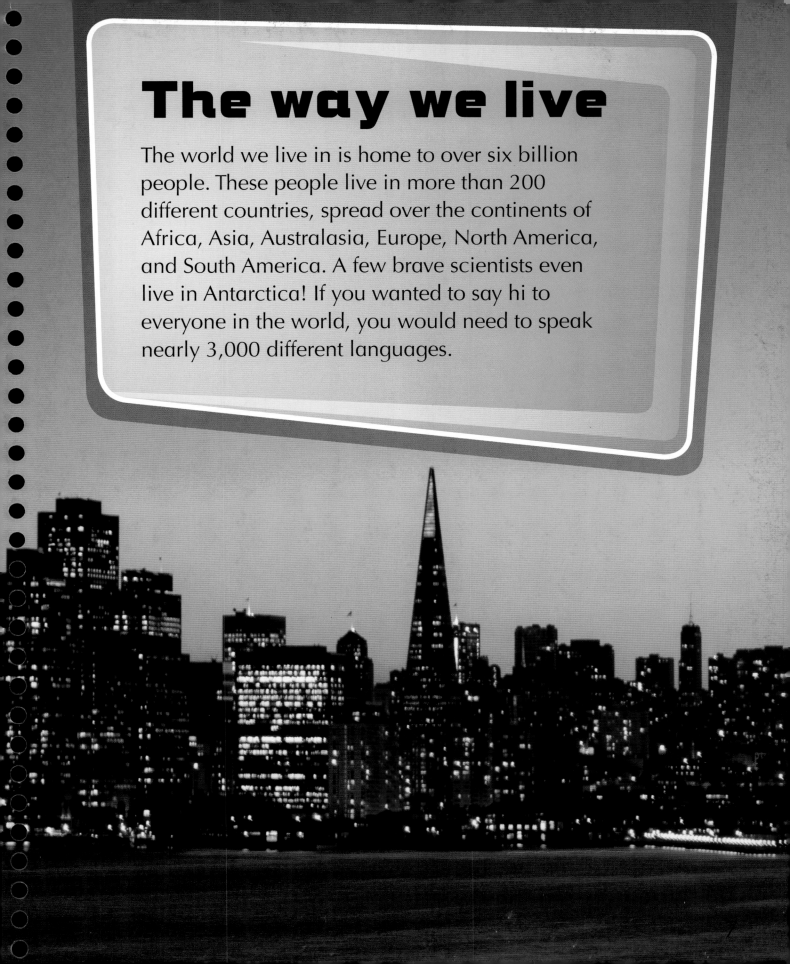

The way we live

The world we live in is home to over six billion people. These people live in more than 200 different countries, spread over the continents of Africa, Asia, Australasia, Europe, North America, and South America. A few brave scientists even live in Antarctica! If you wanted to say hi to everyone in the world, you would need to speak nearly 3,000 different languages.

The houses we live in

Around the world, people live in very different kinds of houses and homes. Some people live in high-rise city apartment buildings, others in tents made of felt.

High homes

Cities are often very crowded, so many people live in apartments. Some of these are in very tall buildings. Hundreds of people may live in one apartment building.

Homes on sticks

In some parts of Southeast Asia, people build houses held up by strong wooden posts. This keeps the house clear of floods—and snakes. It also helps keep the house cool.

Keeping cool

In hot countries, houses have plenty of shady areas to help people stay cool. Houses are often painted white. The white walls reflect, or throw back, the heat of the sun.

Moving homes

Some people do not live in one place all the time. They are called nomads. Nomads usually live in tents that they can take down and carry. The nomads of Mongolia live in round tents called yurts. Yurts have a wooden frame, covered in felt, canvas, and cotton.

Mud houses

In Africa, houses are often made of mud. The mud can be spread over a framework of sticks and allowed to dry. But the mud can also be used to make bricks. It is pressed into brick-shaped boxes and dried in the sun.

9

Our clothes

Clothes may keep us warm or cool. Some clothes are very comfortable, others are trendy or beautiful. Clothes can show that we belong to a particular group, such as a school or a sports team.

Shimmering sari

This beautiful silk dress comes from India. It is called a sari. It is one long piece of material that wraps around the body several times and drapes over the shoulder.

Did you know?

Silk is made by silkworms. These are really caterpillars of the silk moth. They spin a casing, or cocoon, of silk to protect themselves before changing into moths.

Blue jeans

Jeans were created in the United States more than 100 years ago. They are usually made from a strong blue material called denim. Jeans were designed as work pants for miners.

Bright colors

In many African countries, the clothes are often brightly colored. They also have beautiful patterns and special stitching called embroidery. African clothes are usually loose and flowing, to keep people cool in the hot sunshine.

Stay cool

For thousands of years, in the hot Middle East, people have worn long, loose robes. The robes are often white, to reflect the heat of the sun.

At school

In most countries, children are allowed to go to school all year round. But some children have to stop school at certain times of the year to help harvest crops from the fields.

School clothes

In many schools, all the children wear the same kind of clothes as each other, called a uniform. This makes them feel part of the group.

Outdoor school

In countries where it is hot, or the people are poor, school is held outdoors. The children may even sit on the hard ground.

School bus

Children may walk or bicycle to school, or go by car or bus. Often there is a special bus for school children. In snowy places, they may ski or ride on a snow vehicle called a snowmobile.

High-tech schools

In many schools, children have a lot of things to help them learn, such as computers or books. But in some countries, children have to share books, or have no books at all.

Special schools

Some children go to special schools, where they have extra lessons to learn how to dance or sing, or do sports. Other schools help people with special learning needs, such as deaf or blind people.

This is a special school for dance in Thailand.

13

At work

People go to work to earn money so they can pay for their food, clothes, and houses. Most people work during the day, but others, such as doctors and police officers, may work at night.

In an office

Today, a lot of work is done in offices. People sit at a desk with a computer and a telephone. Computers are used for all kinds of office work, from writing letters and e-mails, to doing really difficult math.

Skilled worker

Some people work with their hands to make or fix things. Carpenters work with wood, plumbers work with pipes, and electricians work with electricity.

14

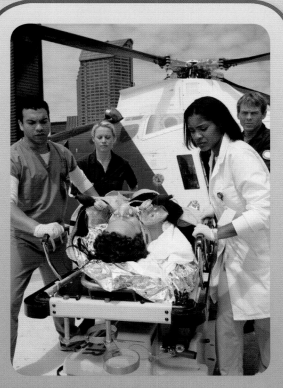

Emergency!

Police, firefighters, and ambulance crews are all part of the emergency services. Their work can often help to save lives. They must always be ready to help at any time of the day or night.

Animal doctor

Veterinarians are trained to work with animals. Some veterinarians need to understand how a lot of different animals' bodies work. Others work with one type of animal, such as horses.

In a factory

People who work in factories make things, such as bicycles. Some of the work might be done by hand, but a lot of it is done by machines.

On the move

In many countries, most people own cars and use them every day. We call this private transportation. Buses, trains, boats, and airplanes are called public transportation. In poorer countries, people still walk or bicycle everywhere.

Animals

When the ground is rough or steep, animals, such as horses or donkeys, often provide the best transportation. In other parts of the world, llamas, water buffaloes, camels, or yaks are used to carry people and things.

Pedal power

An easy way to get around is by bicycle. In China, there are more than one billion bicycles. Some pull carts for carrying shopping bags.

On foot

For many people, walking remains the only way they can travel. Some people have to walk many miles every day to go to school, work, or the market.

Going underground

In large towns and cities, the roads often become jammed with traffic. So some cities have trains that run under the ground. These can carry a lot of people around the city very quickly.

The food we eat

Long ago, people ate only what they could grow, catch, or hunt themselves. Today, supermarkets sell food from all around the world. This means we can eat foods, such as strawberries, all year long, and not just when they are in season.

Preparing food

Food, such as fish, must be cleaned carefully before cooking. This fish has had its head, tail, scales, and bones cut away. The fleshy parts that are left are called fillets.

Steaming

In New Zealand, there are a lot of hot springs and steaming geysers. These underground water sources are naturally hot. The Maoris use the water to cook their food and keep it warm.

18

Takeout

Today, people cook at home less often. We can go out to eat in a café or restaurant. Or we can buy takeout foods, such as pizza or a burger and fries, to eat almost anywhere.

Cooked over a fire

In some areas, people do not have electricity or gas. They cook meals in a big pot over an open fire. It can take hours to collect the firewood.

Based on rice

In eastern countries, many meals include rice. Rice can be steamed and served with a hot, spicy curry, or made with milk and sugar into a dessert. In fact, some people eat rice for breakfast, lunch, and dinner.

Did you know?

One of the most costly foods is caviar. It is the tiny black eggs from a large fish called a sturgeon. The best caviar costs more than a new bicycle. It tastes very salty.

Playing sports

Playing sports keeps you active and healthy. You can play as part of a team, or by yourself. Sports help people to learn about themselves. They learn how to lose without being upset, and how to win without bragging too much. Most of all, sports are fun.

Skiing

Skis allow you to slide over the snow really fast. Sometimes you can even jump through the air.

Choose your sport

Everyone is suited to some kind of sport—even people with disabilities. People in wheelchairs can play and enjoy a wide variety of sports, including archery, basketball, and racing. Some wheelchair athletes compete in marathon races.

20

Soccer

The sport that is played most around the world is soccer. It is a team sport, with 11 players in each team. Every four years the best countries play against each other to try and win the World Cup.

Did you know?

The biggest sporting event in the world is the Olympic Games. These Games happen every four years. Almost 4,000 people take part in more than 25 different sports.

Run and jump

Athletes who run short races very quickly are called sprinters. Sometimes sprinters have to jump over hurdles as well.

21

Music, dance, and art

Most people like to be creative in some way. They might like to sing, dance, play an instrument, or paint. These activities are called the arts. You do not have to be good at the arts—the important thing is to enjoy them.

Break dancers jump around and even spin on their heads.

Break dancing

There are as many kinds of dance as there are music. Some dances are slow and serious. Some, such as break dancing, are very energetic.

Traditional dance

Some types of music and dance are thousands of years old. These Tibetan dancers are performing at one of their summer festivals.

22

Art everywhere

Ever since the first person drew the outline of an animal on a cave wall, people have loved to paint. A few paintings are so valuable that they are kept locked up. Others help to brighten up dull city streets.

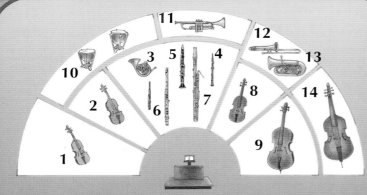

Plan of a modern orchestra

A large group of musicians who play classical music is called an orchestra. Most orchestras have violins (1) and (2), horns (3), oboes (4), clarinets (5), flutes (6), bassoons (7), violas (8), cellos (9), percussion (10), trumpets (11), trombones (12), tubas (13), double basses (14).

This statue is called the Strongman. It is in Japan.

Sculptures

Many artists like to carve figures out of wood or stone. These sculptures can look very real. Around the world, sculptures can be seen in towns and parks as well as in art galleries.

Festivals around the world

In every country of the world, people celebrate special days in different ways. It could be a noisy celebration at the beginning of a new year. Or it might be a religious day when everyone goes to a special place of worship to pray.

Chinese New Year

The Chinese New Year is usually around the end of January or beginning of February. The celebrations traditionally last for 15 days. People dress up and there are a lot of fireworks.

Festival of light

Diwali is the Hindu festival of light. It is celebrated every year between the end of October and the middle of November. Hindus all over the world celebrate by lighting candles.

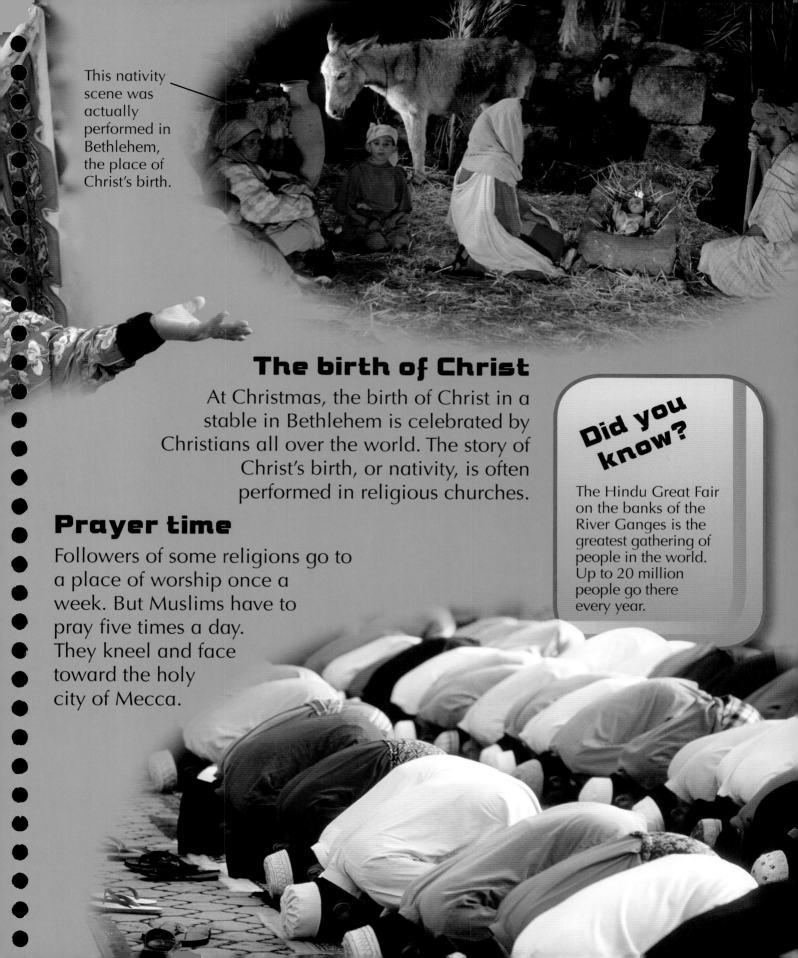

This nativity scene was actually performed in Bethlehem, the place of Christ's birth.

The birth of Christ

At Christmas, the birth of Christ in a stable in Bethlehem is celebrated by Christians all over the world. The story of Christ's birth, or nativity, is often performed in religious churches.

Prayer time

Followers of some religions go to a place of worship once a week. But Muslims have to pray five times a day. They kneel and face toward the holy city of Mecca.

Did you know?

The Hindu Great Fair on the banks of the River Ganges is the greatest gathering of people in the world. Up to 20 million people go there every year.

Governments

Most countries are managed by a group of people called a government. It is the government that makes laws and makes big decisions, such as how much to spend on hospitals, roads, and schools.

Governments meet to discuss things in a special meeting room.

A lot of meetings

The government of a country meets often to debate, or talk, and make decisions. Usually there is one main leader who has the final decision. In the United States this person is called the president.

Voting

In many countries, people choose their leaders and the people they want in the government. They secretly choose and then put their answers in a special box. This is called voting.

Kings and queens

In some countries, the leaders are kings, queens, or emperors. They have power because they are part of an important family. Sometimes the government helps them to run, or manage, the country.

United Nations

Almost every country in the world is a member of a big organization called the United Nations. They meet to resolve arguments between countries and help when there are famines or earthquakes.

Taking over

Sometimes the army may take over a country and make new laws. This is called a coup.

Quick Quiz

Find the correct stickers to answer the questions below.

Which of these homes can be taken down and carried?

apartment
building

yurt

mud house

Answer

Which of these items of clothing was originally designed to be worn by miners?

Answer

blue jeans

sari

school uniform

Which of these is the world's most popular means of transportation?

Answer

car

bicycle

skis

You and your body

Your body is amazing. You can run and jump using your muscles. You can see, hear, smell, touch, and taste with your five senses. And you can solve puzzles with your brain. Your body also does things without you even knowing! All the time—even when you are asleep—your heart is beating, your blood is flowing. And if you hurt yourself, your body quickly tries to make itself better.

Bony parts

Your bones are strong and hard. They hold up the softer parts of your body. Your muscles move your bones. All of your bones together are called your skeleton.

Bone shapes

Different bones have different shapes. The longest bone is your upper leg, or thighbone. The widest bone is your hip. The main bone inside your head is your skull.

Did you know?

A young baby has about 350 bones. As it grows, some of the bones join together. This is why an adult has only 206 bones.

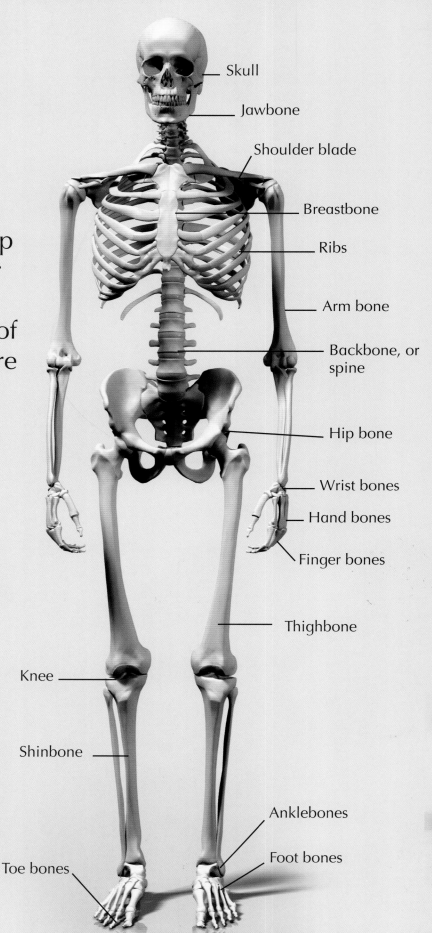

Skull

Jawbone

Shoulder blade

Breastbone

Ribs

Arm bone

Backbone, or spine

Hip bone

Wrist bones

Hand bones

Finger bones

Thighbone

Knee

Shinbone

Anklebones

Foot bones

Toe bones

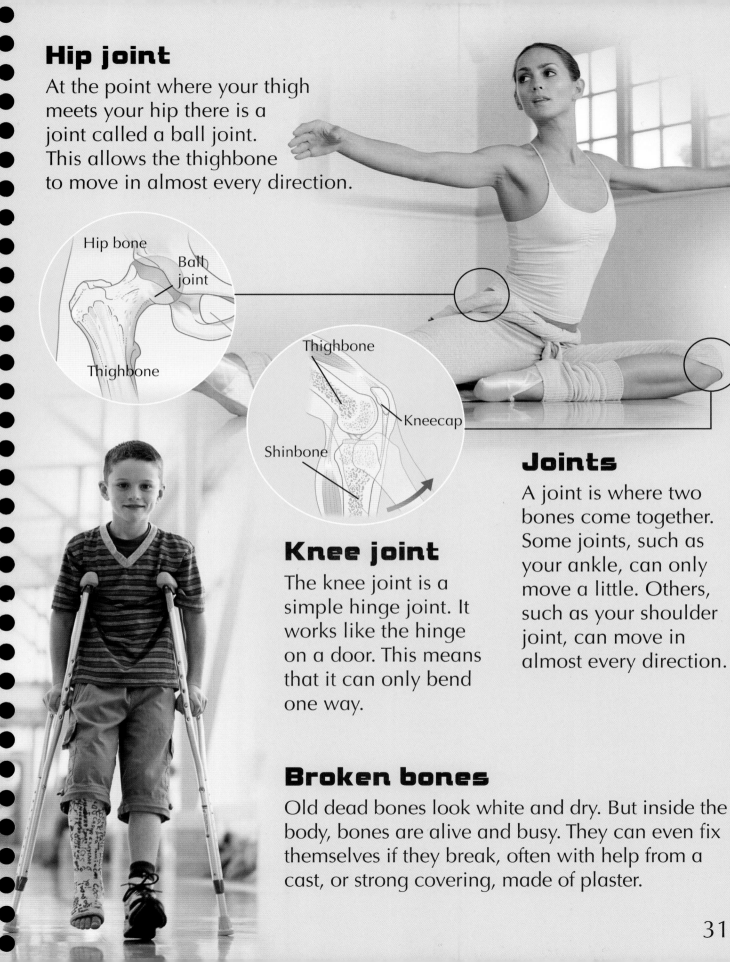

Hip joint

At the point where your thigh meets your hip there is a joint called a ball joint. This allows the thighbone to move in almost every direction.

Hip bone

Ball joint

Thighbone

Thighbone

Knee joint

The knee joint is a simple hinge joint. It works like the hinge on a door. This means that it can only bend one way.

Thighbone

Kneecap

Shinbone

Joints

A joint is where two bones come together. Some joints, such as your ankle, can only move a little. Others, such as your shoulder joint, can move in almost every direction.

Broken bones

Old dead bones look white and dry. But inside the body, bones are alive and busy. They can even fix themselves if they break, often with help from a cast, or strong covering, made of plaster.

31

Muscles

Every time you move, you use your muscles. Even when you are sitting still, your muscles are busy working. You are still breathing and blinking, and your heart keeps on beating. All of these actions use muscles.

Shoulder muscle

Arm muscles

Powerful muscles

Muscles come in all shapes and sizes. Some muscles are large and powerful. Lifting weights can make your muscles stronger.

Did you know?

You have hundreds of muscles in your body—in fact, about 640. Your muscles make up almost half your body weight.

The biggest muscle is in the buttock (butt).

Muscle power

Most muscles are joined to a bone at each end. When the muscle gets shorter, it pulls on the bones and makes your joints move. Usually several muscles pull together for each movement.

The large muscle in your lower leg is called the calf muscle.

The smallest muscle is inside the ear.

Tireless legs

Athletes who run long distances have longer, thinner muscles than weight lifters. These muscles may not be so big, but they can keep working for much longer. This helps the athletes to run long races without tiring.

The longest muscle is across the front of the leg.

Face it

You have more than 60 muscles in your head and around your eyes, nose, and mouth. You use these to make your face move. Try looking surprised, happy, or sad. Can you feel the muscles working?

TOYOTA
281
HELSINKI 2005 ESPOO

On the outside

Your skin covers your body all over. It helps to protect you from small bumps and scrapes, germs, and the harmful rays of the sun. And when your skin does get cut or scratched, it even repairs itself.

Fingerprints

The skin on your hands is covered with lines and creases that help you to hold things tightly. These lines make up little patterns. The ones on your fingertips are called fingerprints. What's amazing about these is that every person's fingerprints are different.

Waterproof

Your skin stops water from getting into your body when you go swimming. But it does let water out through tiny holes called pores. We call this sweating and it helps to cool you down.

Different colors

Skin comes in many different colors, from dark to light. People who live in hot, sunny countries often have darker skins. Darker skins help prevent skin from burning.

Your skin

The tough outside layer of your skin is actually dead. This dead skin rubs off all the time. But new skin is always growing, too. Hairs grow through the skin. They are attached to nerves to help you feel things.

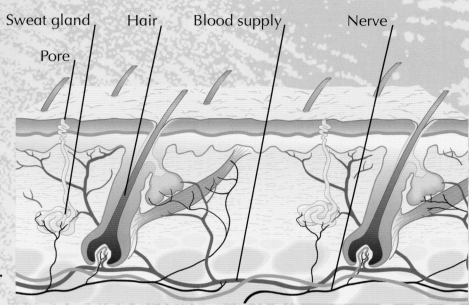

Sweat gland Hair Blood supply Nerve

Pore

Your hair

You have hair all over your body. The tiny hairs on your arms help you feel things. The hair on your head keeps you warm. The color of your hair, and whether it is straight, curly, or wavy, will depend on what your parents' or grandparents' hair is like.

Wavy red hair

Straight blonde hair

Straight brown hair

Curly black hair

Breathing

What do you do all the time, yet hardly ever think about? You breathe—in and out, all day and all night. This is because your body needs a gas called oxygen, which is in the air all around you.

Breathing in, breathing out

As you breathe in, air flows into two spongy bags in your chest called lungs. Your lungs take in the oxygen from the air and release the waste carbon dioxide gas, which you breathe out.

Puffer

People with an illness called asthma often need to use an inhaler, or puffer, to help them breathe more easily.

Your lungs are like two balloons that fill with air when you breathe in.

Air

You need to breathe air all the time. So if you swim underwater, you either have to hold your breath or breathe through a tube called a snorkel.

Snorkel

Windpipe

Lungs

Lungs full

Breathing in

Lungs empty

Breathing out

Voice box

When you talk, sing, or shout, you use your voice box. Air coming up the windpipe from your lungs shakes the voice box to make the sounds. Opera singers train their voices so they can sing loudly.

The lungs

You normally breathe in and out through your nose. As you breathe in, the ribs in your chest move upward and outward. Air passes down your windpipe and fills up your lungs. When you breathe out, your chest moves downward and inward, pushing the air out of your lungs.

Blood

Blood flows all around your body. Pumped by the heart, it never stops moving. Its main job is to carry oxygen, and special substances from food, all around your body.

Blood vessels

Blood vessels are the tubes that carry blood all around the body. Arteries are blood vessels carrying blood with fresh oxygen. Veins carry blood containing waste and carbon dioxide.

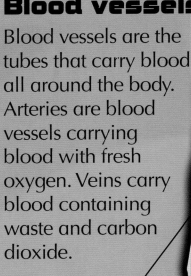

Heart

Artery

Vein

Testing blood

Sometimes when you are sick a nurse may take a few drops of your blood for a test. Blood often carries germs or other signs of illness that can help a doctor understand why you are not feeling well.

38

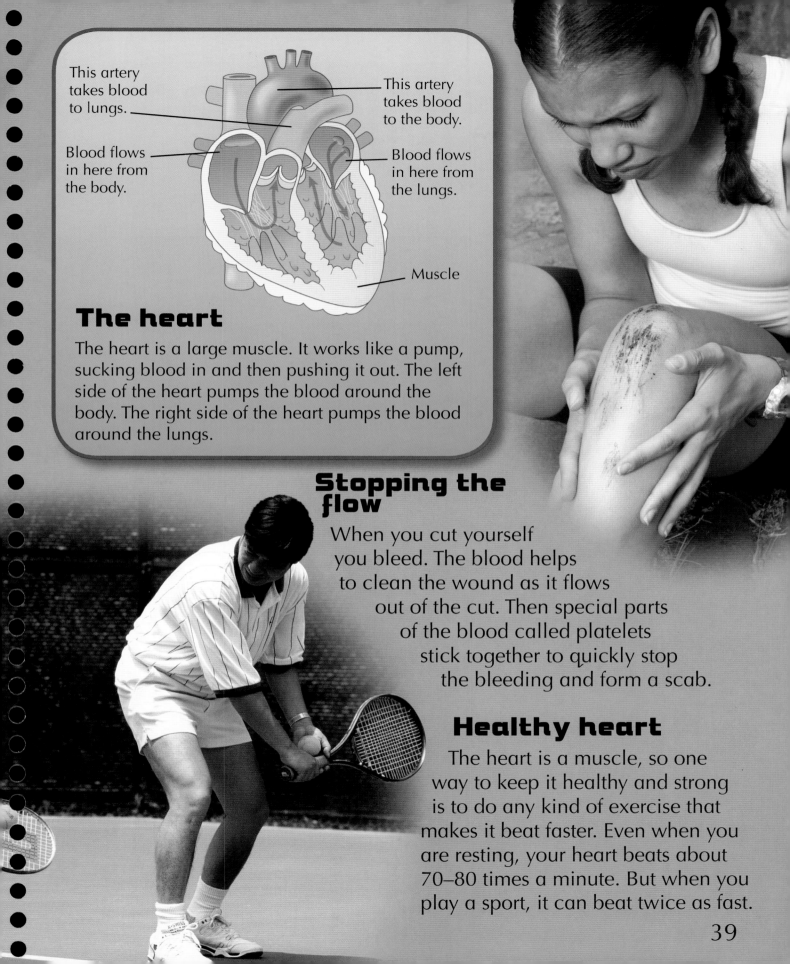

This artery takes blood to lungs.

This artery takes blood to the body.

Blood flows in here from the body.

Blood flows in here from the lungs.

Muscle

The heart

The heart is a large muscle. It works like a pump, sucking blood in and then pushing it out. The left side of the heart pumps the blood around the body. The right side of the heart pumps the blood around the lungs.

Stopping the flow

When you cut yourself you bleed. The blood helps to clean the wound as it flows out of the cut. Then special parts of the blood called platelets stick together to quickly stop the bleeding and form a scab.

Healthy heart

The heart is a muscle, so one way to keep it healthy and strong is to do any kind of exercise that makes it beat faster. Even when you are resting, your heart beats about 70–80 times a minute. But when you play a sport, it can beat twice as fast.

Eating and drinking

Your body needs food and water to work properly. Food contains special substances called nutrients. These give you energy and help your body grow and repair itself.

Why do you eat?

Food gives you more than just the energy to keep you going. It also contains vitamins and minerals. These are special nutrients that help to keep you healthy. That is why you need to eat many different foods.

Lots of water

Nearly two-thirds of your body is made up of water. So you need to drink plenty of water every day. Some foods also contain a lot of water, especially fruit and vegetables, such as melons and carrots. If you get very hot, your body sweats to cool down. Sweat is mostly water. So if you sweat, you need to drink more.

Where does food go?

After you have swallowed your food, it goes down a long tube, called the esophagus, to your stomach. Here special juices take all the goodness out of it. The parts your body cannot use are then passed through more tubes, called the intestine, to your rectum (butt).

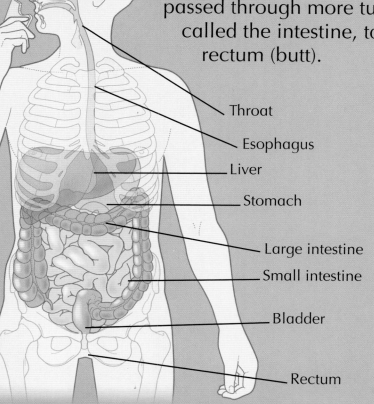

Throat

Esophagus

Liver

Stomach

Large intestine

Small intestine

Bladder

Rectum

How many teeth?

Young children usually grow 20 teeth. From the age of about six, these first teeth fall out, and a new set of 32 adult teeth grows. Teeth need brushing every day to keep them healthy and clean.

On the potty

When you need to get rid of waste food and water you go to the toilet. Babies cannot control when they go, so they wear diapers. Young children who are too small to use the toilet use a potty.

Did you know?

If you could take all the water out of an adult human body, it would fill half a bathtub!

41

Seeing and hearing

You have five senses. These are sight, hearing, smell, touch, and taste. Sight and hearing are perhaps the most important. They allow you to see the world around you, and hear what is going on.

Wide open

Iris Pupil

Light enters the eye through a hole called the pupil. The colored part around it is called the iris. In normal light, the pupil is small (left). In poor light, the pupil gets bigger (right) so that more light is let in.

Too much noise

Your ears hear all kinds of sounds, from a quiet whisper to a huge crack of thunder. But some sounds, such as very loud music, can damage your hearing.

Did you know?

Your ears actually help you to ride a bike! This is because parts of the ear, called the semicircular canals, have nothing to do with hearing. Instead, they help you to balance.

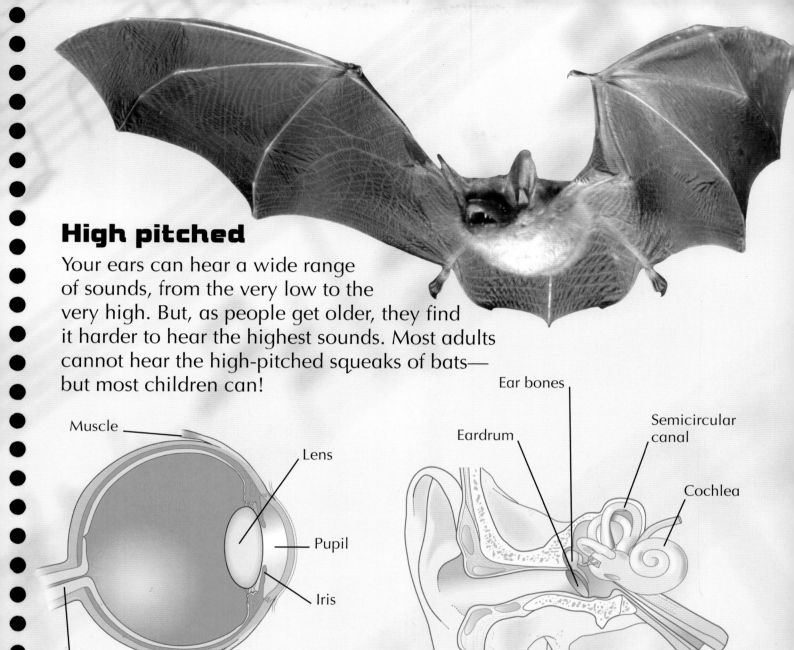

High pitched

Your ears can hear a wide range of sounds, from the very low to the very high. But, as people get older, they find it harder to hear the highest sounds. Most adults cannot hear the high-pitched squeaks of bats—but most children can!

Muscle

Lens

Pupil

Iris

Optic nerve

Ear bones

Eardrum

Semicircular canal

Cochlea

Inside the eye

As light enters the pupil, a lens—just like the lens on a pair of glasses—focuses the light. This makes what you see nice and clear. The eye then sends this picture along the optic nerve to your brain.

Inside the ear

Sounds hit a piece of skin in the ear called the eardrum. They then travel through three tiny ear bones to a snail-shaped part of the ear called the cochlea. From here the sounds travel along nerves to your brain.

Smell and taste

Smell and taste tell you about the foods you eat. They can also warn you of danger. You can smell smoke from a house on fire, long before you feel the heat of the flames. You can taste when food has become rotten before eating enough to give yourself a stomachache.

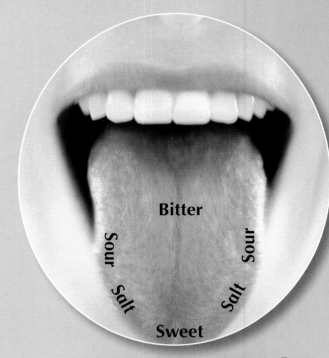

Bitter

Sour

Sour

Salt

Salt

Sweet

Your tongue's taste buds

Your tongue is covered in thousands of taste buds. These are like tiny taste detectors. Taste buds on different parts of the tongue recognize different kinds of taste.

Wide open

Smell and taste often work together. When you bite into an apple, you recognize its taste immediately. But if you shut your eyes and pinch your nose so that you cannot smell, you will not be able to tell an apple from a raw potato!

If you have a bad cold, you may find that all your food tastes the same.

44

Happy smells

Tiny parts of the things you smell float in the air around you. When these tiny parts enter your nose, your brain recognizes them as smells. Lovely smells, such as flower scents, make you feel happy.

Sweet and sour

Young people usually prefer sweet tastes, such as chocolate. As we get older, our tastes change so that we prefer sour, bitter, and even very spicy tastes.

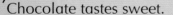

Chocolate tastes sweet.

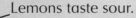

Lemons taste sour.

Nose for hire

Some people use their noses in their jobs. The people who have to pick the best-tasting tea, coffee, and chocolate use their sense of smell more than their sense of taste. People who make perfumes also need a good sense of smell. We call these people "noses."

45

Your brain

If you could see inside your head, you might think that your brain was not very exciting. It looks like pink-gray jelly. But your brain is really amazing, because it controls your whole body. It is also where you think, have ideas, learn, and remember.

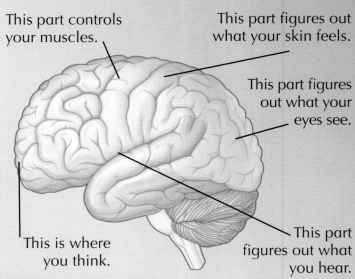

This part controls your muscles.

This part figures out what your skin feels.

This part figures out what your eyes see.

This is where you think.

This part figures out what you hear.

Brain parts

Different parts of your brain do different jobs. The brain also has two sides. The left side controls the right side of your body, and the right side controls the left side of your body.

Left-handed

Most people prefer to write or throw a ball with their right hand. We call them right-handed. But about one person in ten is left-handed. There are also more left-handed boys than girls.

Pain

When you hurt yourself, your nervous system sends messages to your brain to tell it you are in pain. The brain makes you feel pain to warn you that there is a problem.

Problem solving

To play a game such as chess, you use your brain in a lot of ways. You have to learn and remember how to move the pieces. Then you have to figure out what will happen next when you make a move.

Did you know?

As you grow up to become an adult, your body grows about 20 times bigger. But your brain only gets four times bigger.

Learning

To learn, you need to remember things. Your brain can store and find things more quickly than the biggest computer. To play music, you have to remember what the notes mean and where to put your fingers to play them.

Babies and growing up

When a baby is born, we think that it has just started its life. But it has already been growing for nine months inside its mother. The baby grows into a child, then a teenager, and finally an adult.

Before birth

A baby starts its life as a tiny speck, as small as the dot on this "i." Over many weeks, its body takes shape. The baby grows inside its mother's body, in a special part called the womb.

Young children

Young children grow and learn very quickly. Most children can ride a bike, and read and write, by the time they are eight years old.

Adults

Today, more people are living long and healthy lives. Women usually live longer than men, but many people live for 70 years or more. In 2008, the oldest person alive was 115-year-old Edna Parker from Indiana.

Teenagers

Teenagers go through a stage known as puberty. This is when their bodies change to become more like those of adults. By the time they reach 20, they will have stopped growing.

Twins

When two babies are born at the same time we call them twins. Some twins are so similar in appearance that it can be hard to tell them apart. We call them identical twins.

Quick Quiz

Find the correct stickers to answer the questions below.

Which of these parts of the body houses its smallest muscle?

Answer

nose

ear

hand

Which of these parts of the body helps us breathe?

Answer

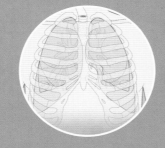
lungs

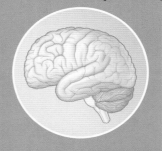
brain

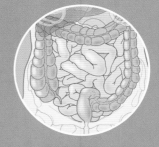
small intestine

Which of these people has the most bones?

Answer

baby

teenager

adult

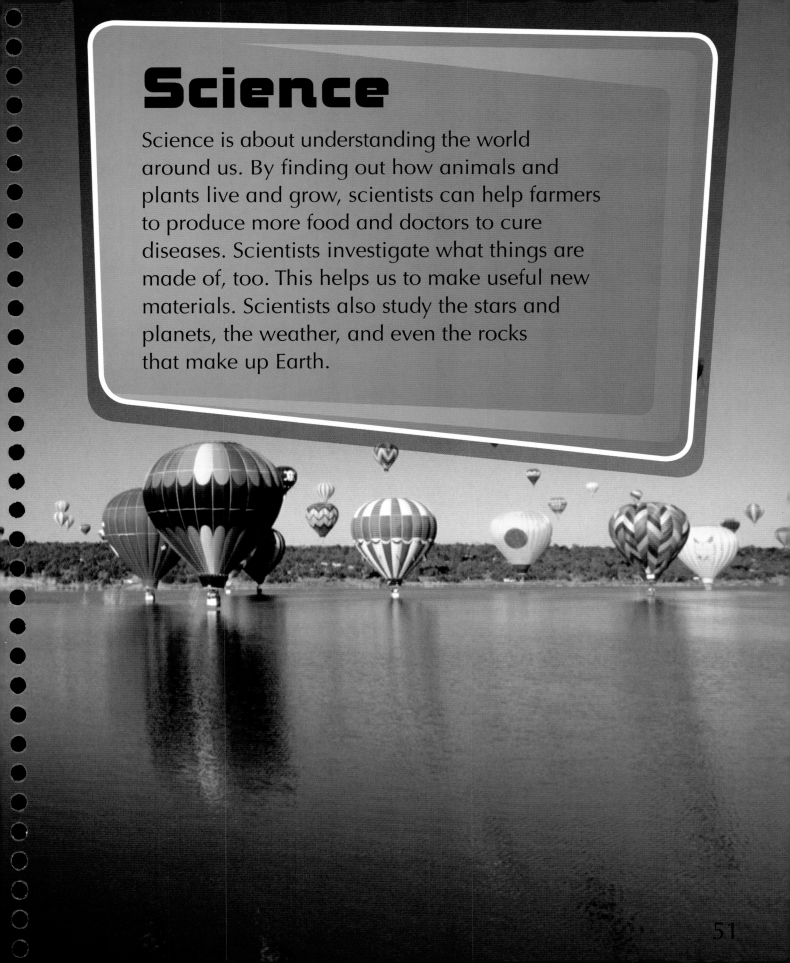

Science

Science is about understanding the world around us. By finding out how animals and plants live and grow, scientists can help farmers to produce more food and doctors to cure diseases. Scientists investigate what things are made of, too. This helps us to make useful new materials. Scientists also study the stars and planets, the weather, and even the rocks that make up Earth.

What is it made of?

Every substance, material, and object in the universe is made up of tiny particles, or pieces, called atoms. There are just over a hundred different kinds of atoms. Some substances, such as gold, contain only one kind of atom, but others, such as plastic, contain atoms of several different kinds.

Too small to see

A microscope magnifies things (makes them look larger). You can use it to look at the dustlike pollen from a flower, or the tiny grains of sand that make up a rock. But atoms are much too small to see, even with a microscope.

Building with atoms

Atoms are like the building blocks of the universe. Just as toy blocks can be snapped together to make all kinds of different shapes, tiny atoms join together in different ways to make all the things we see around us—including our own bodies.

All mixed up

When you mix some substances together, you cannot separate them again. For example, if you mix colored paints, you cannot "unmix" them to get the original colors back.

Easy to separate

Some substances are easy to separate. If you add water to sand you get a squishy mixture. But when sand dries out, you are left with just sand again.

Blue, yellow, and red are called primary colors. You can use them to mix any color you like.

Clothes up close

Your clothes are made up of fibers, or tiny threads, which you can see magnified here. Some are natural fibers, such as wool and cotton. Others, such as nylon, are made from chemicals in factories.

53

Energy

Energy is the ability to make things happen, move, or change. There are many kinds of energy, including light, heat, electricity, and sound. One kind of energy can also change into another.

Energy for life

You need energy to run, jump, shout, breathe, and even think. All your energy comes from the food that you eat. Your stomach breaks down the food to unlock the energy stored inside it.

This car has solar panels that make electricity to drive its wheels.

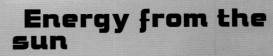

Energy from the sun

Heat from the sun warms the air, land, and sea. Plants use the energy in sunlight to make their own food. Sunlight can also be turned into electricity using solar panels.

Food energy

Sugary foods give us instant energy. Starchy foods, such as pasta, bread, and rice, release their energy more slowly, and keep us going for longer.

Motion energy

Things that move very fast, such as the wind, have a lot of energy. A wind turbine has propeller-like blades that turn in the wind. The turning blades drive a generator that produces electricity.

Fuel energy

Fuels are energy-rich substances that we burn for light and heat, and to power machinery. Coal, oil, and gas are called fossil fuels. They formed millions of years ago from the remains of dead plants and animals.

An oil rig pumps oil from under the sea floor.

Did you know?

The Sun's energy makes life on Earth possible. Heat and light take just over eight minutes to travel from the Sun's surface to Earth.

Solid, liquid, gas

Substances can exist in three different forms. Solids keep their shape and size. Liquids can flow and change shape, but they cannot be squeezed smaller. Gases can flow and change shape. They can also be squeezed smaller or spread out bigger.

Different water

Liquid water flows in rivers and oceans. Water also exists as solid ice, and as a gas called steam.

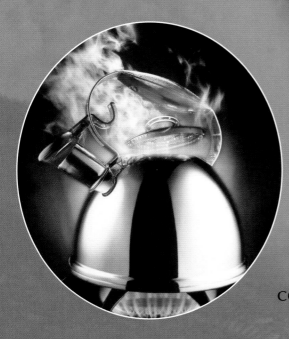

From liquid to gas

When we heat water in a kettle or a saucepan, bubbles of gas form in the water and escape as steam. This change from a liquid into a gas is called evaporation. When a gas cools and turns back into a liquid, it is called condensation.

Floating on air

Air is a mixture of gases, such as nitrogen, oxygen, and carbon dioxide. Some gases weigh less than the gases in air. This airship is filled with a gas called helium. Helium is lighter than air, so the airship floats.

Airships only need small engines because they are so light.

Melt and freeze

If a solid is heated enough, it will turn into a liquid. This is called melting. A glassblower makes vases by blowing air into melted glass. When the glass cools, it becomes solid again.

This glass is so hot it glows red. Heat makes it soft, so it can be shaped.

5

Light and color

We can see objects because light reflects, or bounces, off them and enters our eyes. The most important light source is the sun. Sunlight looks white, but it is really made up of many different colors. Objects look colored because they only reflect some of the colors in sunlight.

Rainbow colors

When the sun comes out during a rain shower, you may see a rainbow. As sunlight shines through small drops of rain in the sky, the raindrops split the white sunlight into its many colors.

Did you know?

We often say there are seven colors in the rainbow: red, orange, yellow, green, blue, indigo, and violet. But these are just the most obvious ones. In fact, a rainbow contains millions of different colors.

Single rainbows are always red on the outside, or top, of their arc.

Making our own light

At night and in dark places, such as caves, we have to make our own light. In the past, people used candles, fires, and oil lamps to see in the dark. Now we have electric lightbulbs in our homes, electric street lamps, and battery-powered flashlights.

Color changers

Colored lights can change the way something looks to us. Even though we know that a banana is yellow, under a blue light it reflects the light's color and so it looks blue.

Mirror image

Smooth, shiny surfaces reflect light best of all. When you look into a mirror, a window, or the surface of calm water, you can see an image of yourself. This is called a reflection. This polar bear is investigating its reflection in the water.

Sound

Sounds are made when objects move rapidly back and forth. This shaking movement is called vibration. Vibrations travel through the air like ripples through water. We hear sounds with our ears.

Making music

Musical instruments have parts that vibrate to make sound. The strings of a guitar vibrate when you pluck them, and the skin on top of a drum vibrates when you hit it. When you blow into a recorder, the air inside it vibrates.

Animal sounds

When you talk, you make sound inside your throat. Many animals make sounds in their throats, too. A leopard roars as a warning. A baby bird chirps to tell its parents it is hungry.

Loud and soft

The harder you bang a drum, the louder the sound it makes. If a sound is too loud, it can damage your ears. This is why people who work with noisy machines wear ear protectors to protect their hearing.

High and low

Some sounds are high or shrill, like a bird singing. We say that they have a high pitch. Other sounds are low and rumbling, like the boom of thunder. These sounds have a low pitch.

Pan flutes have long tubes for low notes, and short ones for high notes.

Forces

A force is a push or a pull. When forces act in different directions, they can make an object move, stop, or change direction. They can also squeeze, squash, stretch, bend, or twist an object to change its shape.

Riding force

You need force to ride a bicycle. The force of your feet pushing on the pedals pulls the chain around and turns the rear wheel. Your hands pull on the hand brakes, while your arms pull on the handlebars to steer.

Balanced forces

Sometimes two forces can balance each other. If two tug-of-war teams pull on the rope with the same force, neither one will move. In the end, usually one side gets weaker and is pulled along by the stronger team.

Scary force

As a rollercoaster races around a track doing loop-the-loops, a force keeps people pressed into their seats, like an invisible safety belt. This force is called centripetal force.

Slowing force

A force called friction tries to slow down objects that slide past each other. There is less friction between smooth surfaces than rough ones. This is why it is easier to sled over smooth snow than over rough gravel.

Down to Earth

People often wish they could fly like birds. But we are kept on the ground by Earth's gravity. This is a downward force that pulls on everything—even birds, which is why they must flap their wings to stay in the air.

Falling fast

When skydivers jump out of a plane, they fall very fast. This is because gravity pulls them down to the ground. When their parachutes open, they catch the air, so the skydivers fall more slowly.

Beating gravity

As a plane moves along the runway, the air rushing over its wings makes an upward force called lift. When lift is greater than the force of gravity, the plane takes off.

Earth's gravity

Everything has gravity—including you! You pull on Earth, just as Earth pulls on you. But gravity depends on size. You are small, so your gravity is weak. Earth is huge, so it has very strong gravity.

Away from Earth's gravity, out in space, everything floats around as if it were weightless.

Did you know?

A rocket has to reach a certain speed to break free of Earth's gravity and get into space. This speed is called "escape velocity." It is 300 times faster than a car speeding along a highway!

Sliding down

The force of gravity is at work in the playground, too. It is gravity that pulls you down a slide. The steeper the slide, the faster you go.

Electricity

Electricity is a kind of energy that flows through wires. We use electricity to create light and heat, and to make machines work. Electricity can also be dangerous—it can even kill.

Skilled work

People who make and repair electrical machines are called electricians and electrical engineers. They know how to work safely with electricity.

Power station

Most of the electricity used in homes, factories, and offices is produced in power stations. The electricity flows along thick cables (wires) carried underground or stretched between tall towers.

Power cable

Power station

How electricity is made

1. Most power stations make electricity from fuels, such as gas, oil, or coal.

2. The gas, oil, or coal is burned to produce steam. The steam is used to drive generators.

3. The generators make electricity, which is carried by cables to our homes and factories.

4. In our homes, we use electricity for heat, light, cooking, and watching television.

Battery power

Batteries are small supplies of electricity that you can carry around. Inside them are chemicals that work together to produce electricity. Batteries power gadgets such as portable game machines and flashlights.

Useful force

Electricity is so useful because it can travel from place to place along wires, and we can turn it on and off. It can power tools, such as drills, sanders, and saws.

Welders use the heat from a spark of electricity to join metals together.

67

Magnets

A magnet creates a special force called magnetism. Magnets can attract (pull toward) and repel (push away) each other. They also attract some metals.

Electromagnet

Crane

Special magnets

Some magnets are made from wire coiled around a piece of iron. These are called electromagnets. When electricity flows though the wire, the iron becomes a strong magnet.

Electromagnets are used to lift scrap iron.

Is it magnetic?

Magnets come in many different shapes, such as bars, horseshoes, and rings. All magnets attract the metal iron, so we say that iron is "magnetic." A refrigerator door is made of steel, which is mostly iron. That is why a refrigerator magnet will stick to it. Cars, paper clips, and some food cans are also magnetic, because they are made of steel.

Giant magnet

The whole Earth is like a giant magnet. Because of this, we can find our way using a magnetic compass. This has a magnetized needle that always lines up to point north–south.

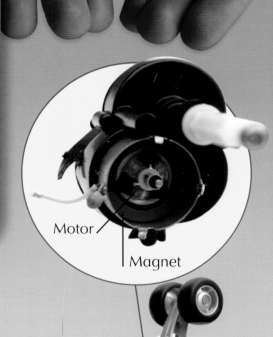

Unlike poles attract

Like poles repel

S N S N   S N N S

Attract or repel?

A magnet's magnetism is strongest at two ends, known as its north pole (N) and its south pole (S). If two magnets are placed with different poles facing each other, they will pull together. If two poles of the same kind are lined up, they will push apart.

Motor

Magnet

Magnets everywhere

Every day we use magnets without knowing. Anything with an electric motor, such as this remote-controlled model car, has magnets inside the motor. The electricity and magnetism work together to make the motor turn.

Materials

Choosing the right material for a job is very important. If you want a cup to drink out of, it has to be waterproof. If you want to build a house, you have to choose materials that are strong, such as bricks or steel.

Tall buildings and bridges are often held up by large steel beams called girders.

Strong

Your body is held up by a skeleton of strong bones. A skyscraper has a skeleton of long beams made of the metal called steel. Steel is strong enough to hold the building up without bending or breaking.

Squishy and stretchy

Some materials, such as a sponge or the bouncy surface of a trampoline, can be squashed or stretched. When you let go, they will quickly spring back into shape.

Tough and colorful

There are hundreds of different plastics. Plastics are very useful materials, because they can be molded into any shape. They also last for a long time and are not harmed by the weather. This is why they are often used to make playground equipment.

Baked hard

Pots, plates, and cups are made from materials called ceramics. These materials are shaped while they are soft and floppy. Then they are baked in an oven to make them hard.

Did you know?

Many kinds of materials can be recycled, or used again. They include glass, metals, paper, and plastic. Recycling helps the environment as less garbage ends up in dumps.

Quick Quiz

Find the correct stickers to answer the questions below.

Which of these is a primary color?

green

purple

red

Answer

Which of these objects can help people find their way?

Answer

compass

battery

trampoline

Which of these objects can generate electricity?

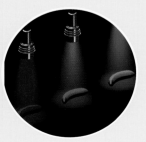
colored light

wind turbine

hot air balloon

Answer

Machines and gadgets

We build machines and gadgets to help us to do things. Some machines, such as a can opener, are simple. Others, such as a jumbo jet, which has over six million parts, are amazingly complicated. Some machines, such as jet skis, only really help us to enjoy ourselves! Gadgets are usually little devices that do something interesting. Many gadgets, such as cell phones, can be both very useful and a lot of fun.

Simple machines

Machines make it easier for us to do things, or help us do things we could not do at all. Some of the most useful machines, such as ramps, levers, and wheels, are also really simple.

Ramps

Ramps are sometimes used instead of stairs or escalators. They help people to move from one level to another. They are useful for people with wheelchairs, luggage, or strollers.

Gears

Gears are the toothed wheels that your bicycle chain wraps around. Usually there is one big gear wheel attached to the pedals, and one or more smaller gear wheels attached to the back wheel. Having gears of different sizes at the back makes it easier for you to ride your bicycle up and down hills.

Chain

Teeth

Wheels

Wheels help us to move or carry heavy loads. Some wheels are tiny. Others are over 10 feet high. Bigger wheels make it easier for heavy trucks to travel over rough ground without getting stuck in the mud.

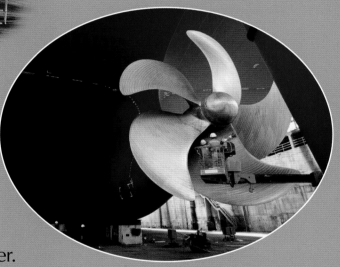

Screws

Screws change a turning motion into a forward or backward motion. If you turn a wood screw with a screwdriver, it forces its way forward into the wood. A ship's propeller is also a kind of screw. As it turns, it pushes the ship forward through the water.

Levers

A lever can help us to lift things that would usually be too heavy for us. The seesaw is a lever that allows you to lift your partner into the air.

To use a lever, you have to rest it on something. The point where it rests is called the fulcrum.

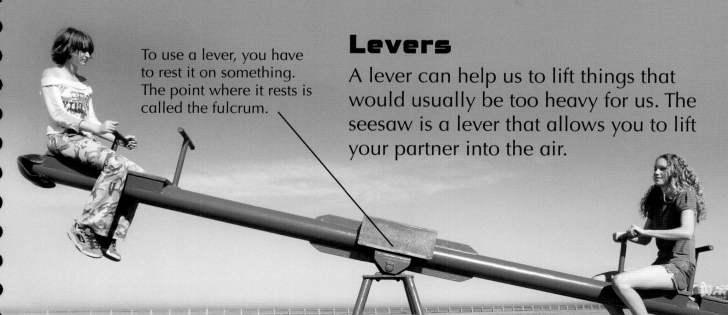

75

In the home

Kitchens have many machines and gadgets. They help us to prepare and cook our food. We also use machines to keep our homes and our clothes clean. Most machines are powered by electricity.

Drum

Vacuum cleaners

Vacuum cleaners use an electric motor to create powerful suction. The suction pulls the dirt and dust into the vacuum.

Dust and dirt are sucked up into this container.

This vacuum cleaner has a big ball instead of wheels to make it easier to push.

Washing machines

Washing machines have a large drum that is turned by a big electric motor. Holes in the drum let the water in and out to wash the clothes. When it is washing, the drum turns backward and forward slowly.

Did you know?

Over 100 years ago there was no electricity. People worked all their machines by hand. Imagine life without a washing machine and a vacuum cleaner.

Food processors

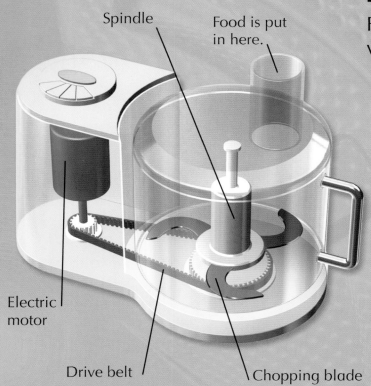

Spindle

Food is put in here.

Electric motor

Drive belt

Chopping blade

Food processors can prepare vegetables or mix ingredients much faster than can be done by hand. They have an electric motor that turns a spindle very fast. Sharp blades for chopping, or beaters for mixing, can then be attached to the spindle.

Two in one

A can opener is two machines in one. The lever part pushes the blade onto the can. The blade is a wedge that then cuts a long hole around the top of the can.

ON
O
OFF

High-speed juicers

Juicers have very powerful motors. Blades chop and shred the fruit or vegetables into a soft mushy mixture called "pulp." The pulp is then pushed through a strainer to squeeze out all the juice.

Tools for the job

Whatever the job, from drilling a hole to making a baseball bat, there is a tool that is made to do it. Many tools are powered by electric motors—but a few still need muscle power.

Flying sparks

A grinder has a hard spinning disk that can be used to smooth, shape, or cut things. When it grinds metal, sparks and sharp parts of metal fly in all directions.

Lathes

A lathe is a special machine for making shapes out of wood or metal. Baseball bats, candlesticks, and bolts can be made with a lathe. To make a bat, the wood is held at one end of the lathe and spun around. A cutting tool is then held against the wood to shape it.

Electric motor

Chuck

Drill bit

Rechargeable batteries

Trigger switch

Inside an electric drill

An electric drill has a powerful motor inside. The drill "bit" is the part that makes the hole. It has a sharp tip and a spiral groove to carry away the material being drilled away. The bit is held tightly in metal jaws called the chuck.

Did you know?

The fastest drills can spin around more than 1,000 times every second. That is 60,000 times a minute!

Small but sharp

A saw has small, sharp teeth. The teeth are bent alternately to each side, first one way, then the other. This makes the saw cut a wide slot, and stops it from getting stuck.

Saw teeth

On the farm

Farms once employed a lot of people to work on the land and care for the animals. Today, big machines do many of the jobs people once did. And as farms have gotten bigger, so, too, have the machines.

Plow

Plowing time

Plows are like big curved spades that dig and turn over the soil all at once. They are pulled by big tractors with powerful engines. Plowing helps to bury weeds and let air into the soil.

V750

Milking machine

When cows were milked by hand, the job used to take all morning. Today, milking machines can milk a whole herd of cows in less than an hour.

Spraying apples

Helicopters and airplanes are sometimes used to spray crops to keep them healthy. But many farmers are trying not to use so many chemicals and to grow crops more naturally. This is called organic farming.

Combine harvester

A combine harvester does several jobs. First it cuts the wheat. Then it "threshes" it to separate the grain from the waste. The waste straw is thrown out the back as the combine moves along. The grain is stored until it can be unloaded, when it is pushed through a long tube into a trailer.

LEXION 570
Terra-Trac

The grain is stored here.

Cab

Grain tube for unloading.

Cutter

Waste straw comes out of here.

The grain is separated from the waste here.

At the building site

Long ago, people put up buildings using their own muscles and a few simple tools. Today, a building site is full of huge, powerful machines. With their help, a tall skyscraper can be built in just three months.

Lifting

A tower crane lifts heavy loads around the building site. As the building gets taller, extra parts have to be added to the crane's tower, so it gets taller, too.

Bulldozer blade

Flattening

A bulldozer uses its big blade to push huge piles of earth and flatten the ground. It moves along slowly on big metal caterpillar tracks.

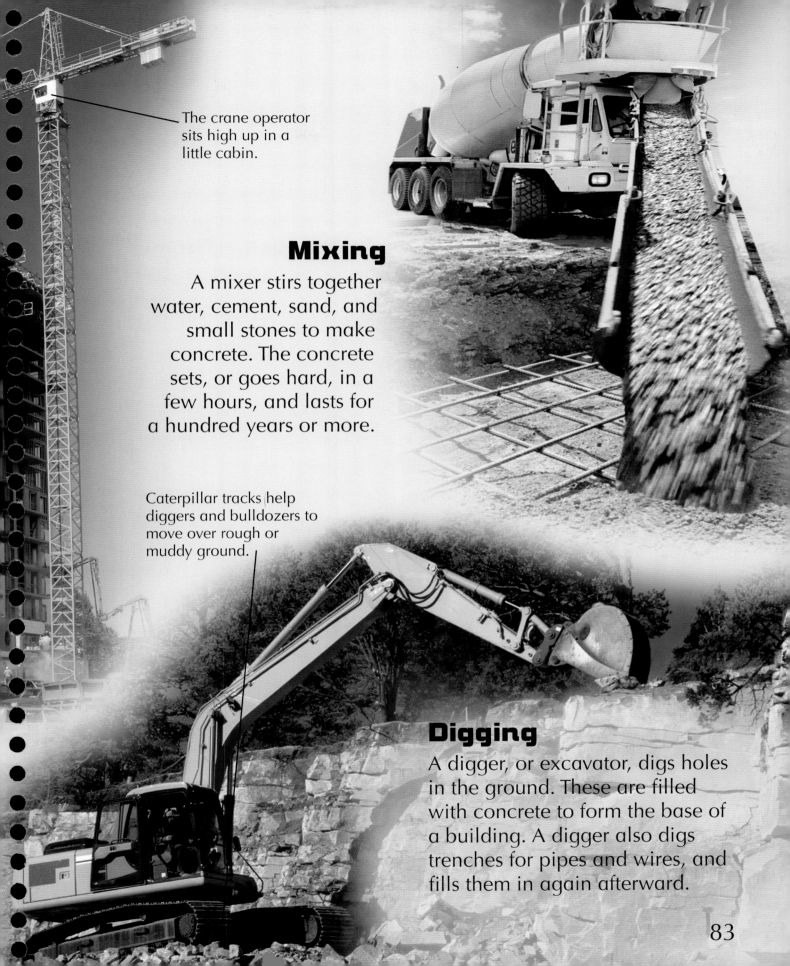

The crane operator sits high up in a little cabin.

Mixing

A mixer stirs together water, cement, sand, and small stones to make concrete. The concrete sets, or goes hard, in a few hours, and lasts for a hundred years or more.

Caterpillar tracks help diggers and bulldozers to move over rough or muddy ground.

Digging

A digger, or excavator, digs holes in the ground. These are filled with concrete to form the base of a building. A digger also digs trenches for pipes and wires, and fills them in again afterward.

On the road

Our roads are busy with
machines we call vehicles.
There are cars, motorcycles,
trucks, and buses.
They take people,
loads, and cargoes
from one place
to another.

This electric car is not
only quiet and clean,
it also goes very fast.

Electric cars

Most cars have
gasoline or diesel engines.
An electric car has big
batteries that power an electric
motor. It is quiet and wastes
less energy than a
gas-engined car.

Double bus

Articulated buses are like two buses
joined together. They can carry more
people around crowded cities—but
they only need
one driver.

On two wheels

A motorcycle is small and fast. But it can only carry one or two people. Some racing bikes can travel more than 185 miles an hour.

Did you know?

There are around a billion cars in the world. Ten new ones are made every second.

Tractor-trailer

The biggest trucks are called tractor-trailers. They have a separate cab and engine at the front, called a tractor, and a big load-carrying trailer at the back.

Trailer

Tractor

KENWORTH

Going by train

Trains run on metal railroad lines called tracks. Passenger trains stop at stations so people can get on and off. Freight trains carry all kinds of loads, from coal and sand, to packages and cars.

Bullet trains

Japan has some of the fastest trains in the world. Known as "bullet trains," they can travel at speeds of nearly 185 miles an hour.

Bullet train

Signals

Where a road crosses a railroad line, there is usually a barrier and lights to warn drivers when a train is coming. Trains can change onto a different track at special places called "switches." The rails slide sideways to join another line and make the train change direction.

Only one rail

Train systems that have just one rail in the middle are called monorails. These trains are usually found in cities, airports, and docks.

Did you know?

Trains called maglevs use magnetism to float above, and glide along, a single track. Some maglevs can go more than 300 miles an hour.

Overhead wires

Some electric trains have motors at both ends, and even in the middle. These motors get their electricity from overhead wires that the train touches as it goes along.

Power cables

In the air

The quickest way to travel a long way is to fly. In less than a day, you can fly to the other side of the world. You begin and end your flight at an airport, where the airplanes take off and land.

A lot of people

The biggest jumbo jets carry more than 500 people, as well as all their luggage. They can also carry enough fuel to fly halfway around the world without stopping.

Hover

Helicopters can take off and land without a runway. They can also "hover," or stay still in one place, in the sky. This makes them useful for all kinds of jobs, including fire fighting and rescuing people from the sea.

This fire department helicopter is dropping water on a forest fire.